DRAWING MAGIC

HELEN PLUM MEMORIAL LIBRARY

P9-DMS-299

Helen Plum Library
Lombard, IL

NORTH LIGHT BOOKS
CINCINNATI, OH

Y
743,6
DRA

Drawing Magic. Copyright © 2001 by GE Fabbri. Manufactured in China. All rights reserved. The patterns in this book are for the personal use of the reader. By permission of the publisher, they may be hand-traced or photocopied to make single copies, but under no circumstances may they be resold or republished. No other part of this book may be reproduced in any form or by any electronic or mechanical means including information storage and retrieval systems without permission in writing from the publisher, except by a reviewer, who may quote brief passages in a review. Published by North Light Books, an imprint of F&W Publications, Inc., 1507 Dana Avenue, Cincinnati, Ohio 45207. (800) 289-0963. First edition.

Visit our Web site at www.artistsnetwork.com for information on more resources for artists.

04   03   02   01   00   5   4   3   2   1

A catalog record for this book is available from the U.S. Library of Congress.

ISBN 1-58180-230-7

American Editor: Diane Ridley Schmitz
Editorial Production Manager: Kathi Howard
Production Supervisor: Sara Dumford
American Designer/Production: Kevin Martin
Studio Manager: Ruth Preston

3 1502 00526 3080

Contents

Part 1: Drawing Fur, Feathers, Fins and Scales

5

Draw a Pet Dog

6

Hop To It!

9

Pretty Kitty

11

Draw a Perfect Pony

14

Eagle Head

16

It's a Hoot!

19

Chirpy Chicks

21

Dashing Dolphins

23

Sea Cow Wow!

25

Ray Okay

27

Scaly Fish

29

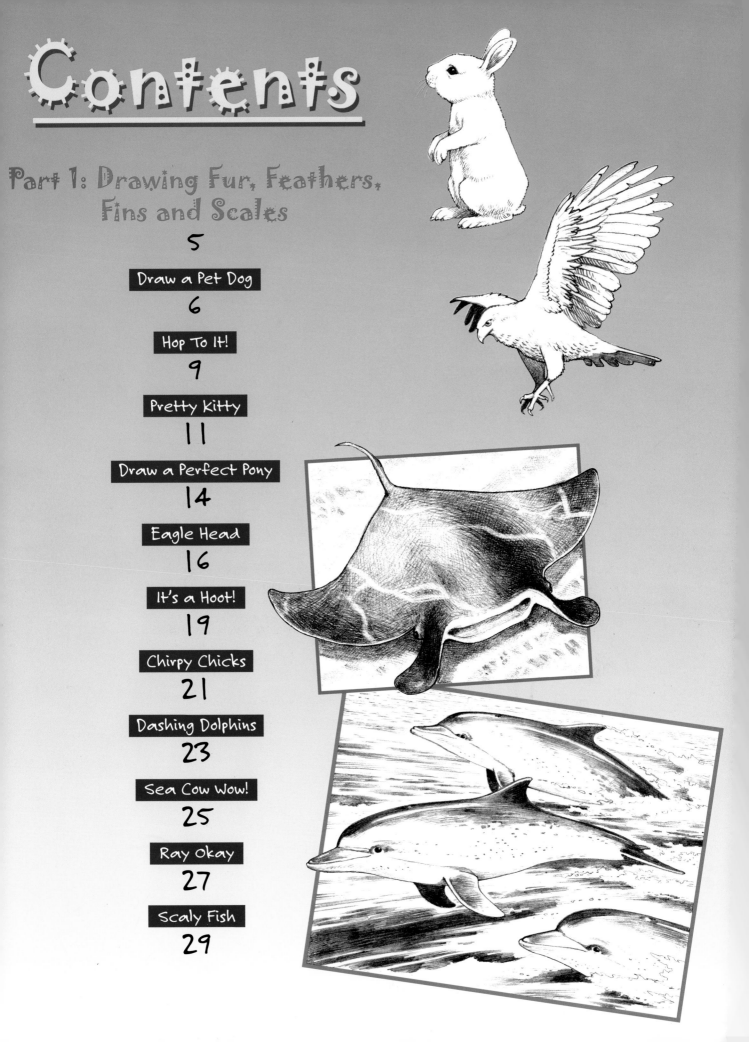

Shark Attack!
32

Snap to It!
35

Dragon Flight
38

Part 2: Drawing Scary Stuff, Speed and Space

41

Scary Bats!
42

Fierce Fangs!
44

Draw Spooky Ghosts
47

Spooky Tree
49

Creepy Castle
52

Fast Forward
55

Fast Track
58

Jet Away!
61

Blast Off!
63

Part 1

Drawing Fur, Feathers, Fins and Scales

Sketch book

You'll need a 2B pencil, eraser, sharpener and crayons or colored pencils

Draw a pet dog

No two dogs look exactly alike. Their hair can be shaggy, short, wiry or woolly. See how many different types you can draw.

It's a wonder this big dog can see where she's going with all that long, shaggy hair! Compare how she looks to the puppy beside her — his coat is short and wiry. Drawing dogs like these is easy when you start with simple shapes like circles and rectangles. Have a look at the dogs that live near you and then try drawing them.

ha ha!

What's worse than raining cats and dogs?

Hailing a taxi!

FUN FACTS

Although today's pet dogs are tame, actually they are descended from wild wolves. Over the last thousands of years dogs have been bred and trained to do lots of different types of work, such as hunting, herding sheep and guarding property. These days they are also used to search for people who are lost in snow or dense undergrowth, and they can be trained to sniff out drugs and bombs. As well as working as guide dogs for the blind, dogs can now be trained to help deaf people, too.

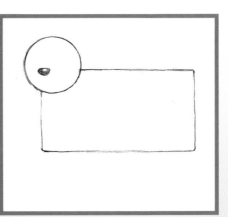

...Now draw it step by step

1 Lightly draw a rectangle for the shape of the big dog's body. Add a circle for the head and a shiny black nose with a little white highlight on it.

2 Draw the shape of the body, head and left legs using a slightly ragged line. Add a mouth and tongue, and a line on both feet to look like claws.

3 Add the right legs and draw some long, shaggy hair on the face, neck and front leg. Draw a rectangle and square to start off the puppy.

4 Following the Quickdraw on the right, draw in the puppy. Add a patch on his back and a few zigzags for a short coat. Give the big dog some more fur.

5 Shade in some fur on the insides of the big dog's legs. Add some more short fur and shading on the small dog. Draw in the ground and background.

Color it!

Once you've drawn your dog in pencil, you can color it using colored pencil or paints. Start by making the tongue pink. Add some brown hair around the mouth and a few dark grey areas on the back of the head and shoulder. Don't worry if your coloring overlaps your pencil lines. This will help make the hair look shaggy. To give the fur more texture, add some blue and grey lines. Now go over some of the pencil lines with black paint and a fine brush, or a fine colored pencil. Color in the shadows, in grey, under the chin and on the tongue. Then, go over the nose again with black, but leave the whitish highlight on the end, as this makes it look round and wet! Now color the dog's body in the same way.

Different dogs!

To draw the heads of different dogs, start with a square or circle. Look closely at the dog's eyes — are they big and round, or small and oval? What are the ears like? Now see how you can change the pencil lines to show their different coats.

Rusty the Chow Chow has a very thick coat, drawn with small, crinkly lines.

For a long-haired Borzoi like Lucy, use lots of long, wavy lines.

Rows of tiny lines give Rex the Staffordshire Bull Terrier his short hair.

Schnauzer dogs like Timmy have thick, bushy hair under their nose and chin.

Feathery and wavy lines make an elegant hairstyle for a Poodle like Nina.

The shaggy hair of Scampy the Yorkshire Terrier needs lots of long, curving lines.

Quickdraw
...a puppy

Start with a large oval the body a a small ova for the he

Draw in the neck and the shape of the head, with short, tufty hair on top. Add the mouth, nose, ears, tail and legs.

Draw aro the body with a ragged lir Add eyes claws and patches o the head and back. erase the guideline:

Draw more fur on the chest, legs and face. Finally, shade the head, back and inside leg, using short dark lines.

DRAWING ✓
SHADING ✓
COLORING ✓

Sketch book

Hop to it!

You'll need a 2B pencil, eraser, sharpener and whatever you like to color with!

Can you make Floppy, the fluffy bunny, look this cute? Sharpen your pencil and have fun trying!

This pet picture is full of detail and texture, but it's easy to draw. The fluffy bunny is made up of simple shapes and lots of tiny, shading strokes that fan out from its twitchy nose. A comfy bed of straw is built up with crisscrossed lines and dark shading. It's easy to make the wood at the back of the hutch look real — all it takes is long, flat ovals and short, vertical dashes to create the knots and grain.

FUN FACTS

The most common type of wild rabbit in North America is the cottontail. Cottontails have brown speckled fur but are named for their short white tails which look just like a ball of cotton. Another trait of the cottontails is their ability to sit without moving for hours on end! This is to avoid being noticed when it senses danger. The black-tailed jackrabbit is one rabbit that doesn't sit still but uses quickness to escape their enemies. They can achieve speeds up to 45 mph and leap as far as 15 to 20 feet!

ha ha! where do rabbits go when they get married? On their bunnymoon!

...now draw it step by step

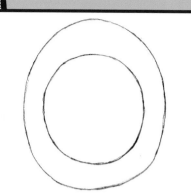

1 Start by lightly drawing a large circle for the body in the center of your page. Add a smaller circle inside this for the rabbit's head.

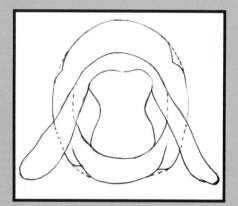

2 Add four dimples to the body. Sketch two ears that join at the top of the head. Add curved cheek lines down each side of the rabbit's face.

3 For the nose and mouth, draw an **X** shape. Give the bunny a furry outline. Add a pair of dark eyes and shade the ears. Start drawing the straw.

4 Give the rabbit whiskers. Add short lines for fur on the face and body. Draw a horizontal line behind the rabbit and build up the straw.

5 For the wooden hutch background, draw long, flat ovals, then wavy lines flowing around them. Add short, upright lines all over.

Quickdra
...a baby rabb

Follow these simple steps t sketch a begging bunny!

Draw a circle for the head on top of a stretched body shape. Inside this, add a curved line for a haunch.

Sketch in the nose. Give the rabbit front legs, its other haunch, a little bobtail and long, flat feet.

Outline the eye. Then draw the paw details and long, pointy ears. Shape the back and shade the furry belly.

Finish off the fur under the head and legs. Shade the eye and inside the ear, then add whiskers.

DRAWING ✓
SHADING ✓
SPONGE PAINTING ✓
PAINTING ✓

Pretty kitty

You'll need a 2B pencil, sharpener, eraser, paintbrush, paints, waterproof black felt-tip pen and a small sponge.

Meow! Smokey the kitten thinks her toy mouse may scuttle away. Sketch this furry feline before she pounces!

This purr-fect puss is easy to draw! Sketch her fur with short lines that follow her shape. The longest fur is on her back and inside her ears. Shade oval-shaped pupils in her eyes to give her a look of real cat concentration. Draw patterns of darker fur on Smokey's face and give her long whiskers – don't forget the ones above her eyes! Leave her paws white and shade her tail solid black. Finally, add the finishing touches to the tiny, toy mouse, ready for some squeaky fun!

FUN FACTS

Because of their intelligence and independence, cats are one of the world's most popular pets. They are part of a large, meat-eating family of mammals that includes tigers, leopards, lions and panthers. It is thought that the first cats were domesticated by the Egyptians as long ago as 3500BC! These pussies became pampered pets and were honoured in many paintings and sculptures. Some were even mummified! In the Middle Ages, European cats were often associated with witchcraft and the supernatural. Today, a black cat is seen as a symbol of good luck.

ha ha!
what do cats like to read?
Mews-papers!

...now draw it step by step

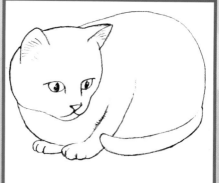

1 Start by drawing a large, potato shape for the body. On the left side, draw a circular head with a point at the base for the mouth and nose.

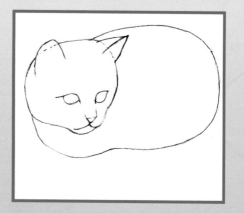

2 Draw the ears. Outline the eyes, with lines pointing down towards a tiny, triangular nose. Sketch two curves below the nose for the mouth.

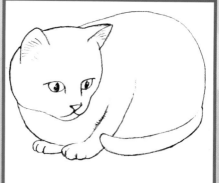

3 Sketch fur in the ears. Shade pupils in the eyes, leaving white dots. Draw a leg from the middle of the body and add the paws. Draw the tail.

4 Draw bands of short hair on the face, across the body and along the tail. Shade the tail, then add a shadow on the ground. Draw the toy mouse.

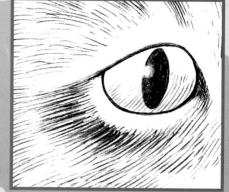

5 Lightly shade the eyes. Build up fur around them with short strokes. Make some patches dark and some light to show the patterns in the fur.

Quickdra
...a kitten

This beautiful, white kitte full of fun and can be pre mischievous, too!

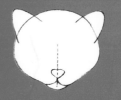

Draw a circle with a point base. Add a nose and a cur mouth. Outline the ears

Add fur in the ears draw the e Sketch front l making left one lon Add claws a furry ch

Shape furry-edged back legs and an upright tail. Put dots on either side of the nose.

Shade sh patche fur on underside the b and back l Add whisk and lig shade the e and the no

Paw show

Check out the different shapes and colors of these furry friends. They were drawn with a black, waterproof felt-tip pen, then colored in with watercolor paints for purr-leasing results!

Persian

The most popular of the long-haired breeds, the Persian cat comes in many different shades. It has a shaggy coat and a snub nose.

Lynx

This is the only untamed puss of the pack. It lives out in the wild and has never been domesticated.

Siamese

This slender aristo-cat can make a howling meow. It has a creamy-colored chest and a chocolate-brown face and lower body.

Burmese

Here's a real show cat, with its sleek coat and large, green eyes. These cats were first brought over from Burma in 1930.

Ginger

Long-haired cats can be quieter and more timid than their short-haired relatives. This ginger tomcat spends a lot of time asleep!

Pet painting

The Ancient Egyptians loved their cats so much that they even gave them jewellery to wear! Try painting your own antique puss picture. Draw a cat outline with a waterproof felt-tip pen. Then, mix up some brown and orange paint and sponge it on to the paper. When this is dry, use a fine paintbrush to go over the cat shape again with dark brown paint. Finally, mix a creamy yellow and carefully paint another outline. Don't forget the earring!

Sketch book

Draw a perfect pony

Drawing this handsome pony is easy if you build up the lines and shading gradually.

You'll need a 2B pencil, eraser, sharpener, ruler and whatever you like to color with!

Here's your chance to draw a beautiful, frisky pony. See how sweeping pencil lines make his mane and tail look long and flowing, while careful use of short lines give his smooth coat a real gleam. By giving him pricked ears he looks especially alert. Looking as good as this, the pony here could come away from a horse show with a shiny, silver cup.

FUN FACTS Some of the most famous ponies in the world belonged to the Pony Express postal service which started in the Wild West in 1860. The ponies took over from stagecoaches to transport mail between Missouri and California, cutting delivery time from six weeks to just eight days! Each pony and its rider could speed across 75 miles of countryside in a day before handing the mailbag over to the next team.

...now draw it step by step

1 Lightly draw a long oval as a guide for your pony's body, making one end slightly fatter. Add a smaller oval for the head and draw two slightly curved lines for the neck.

2 Draw the pony's body and head over the guidelines. Take care with the shape of the back, muzzle and cheek. Add the mouth and the tops of the left legs. Erase the guidelines.

3 Add details such as alert ears, an eye and nostrils. Note the lines above the eye, below the cheek and down the neck. Draw the other two legs and add fetlocks and hooves.

4 Draw a line to define the hindquarter, plus tiny, curved lines on the hocks of the hind legs. Add a mane and tail, and shade inside the legs. Use a ruler for a fence and add grass.

5 Use the same tiny lines to shade parts of the body. You don't need to shade the whole body. Leaving white areas will make the coat look glossy. Draw a lovely long-haired tail.

6 Make the mane and tail darker and thicker with lots of overlapping lines. Use long, bold pencil strokes from the back of the neck to make the hair fly in the wind.

7 Shade the lower legs, as well as the grass under the pony to create a shadow on the ground. Finally, add some fence posts and fill in the bushes in the background.

ha ha!
Why did the pony eat with its mouth open?

Because it had bad stable manners!

15

Sketch book

Eagle head

Learn how to draw this powerful bird of prey. Layers of feathers give the eagle its beautiful coat - and make it such an expert flyer too!

You'll need a 2B pencil, an eraser and a steady hand!

To show that the eagle's chest is puffed out, space the feathers wider apart in the middle and closer together at the edges. Draw a line down the middle of each feather. Shade the right-hand side of each feather with dark sketchy lines to make the barbs. This shading will make the chest look rounded. Draw much smaller, pointier feathers on the eagle's head. Overlap them closely. The bird's beady eye should hold your gaze when you look at the picture. Use the end of the eraser to create a shiny highlight on the pupil. This will make the eye look bright and alert.

FUN FACTS

Eagles are some of the largest birds in the world. They can weigh up to 20 pounds and have a wingspan as big as 8 ft. They are birds of prey which means they are hunters and meat-eaters. There are about 60 species of eagles, living mostly in Africa and Asia. In the wild, they can live 20 to 30 years, in captivity they may survive for up to 50 years. The bald eagle is not really bald at all! Its head is covered with white feathers which give the bird its unusual look! And the only golden bit of the golden eagle is a patch of golden feathers on the back of its neck!

ha ha!
Why do birds fly south in summer? Because it's too far to walk!

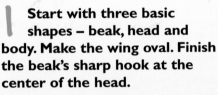

Quickdraw
...an eagle

To create this flying eagle, follow our step-by-step guide.

Lightly outline the eagle's head, body and tail.

Sketch in beak and brow lines. Outline the powerful legs and large wing.

...now draw it step by step

1 Start with three basic shapes – beak, head and body. Make the wing oval. Finish the beak's sharp hook at the center of the head.

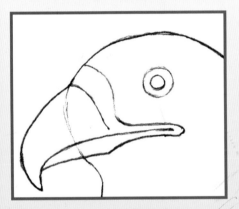

2 Add extra lines to the beak. Draw a double circle for the eye, positioning it midway between the beak and the top of the head.

3 Draw the brow line over the eye to give the eagle its mean look. Sketch in the zigzag line between the head and chest feathers.

Draw the talons – front foot first! Build up the feathered outline, and erase the guidelines.

4 Shade the eye and beak. Give the head a jagged, feathery outline. Build up a few layers of chest and wing feathers – they look a bit like scales.

5 Draw the smaller head feathers all in one direction. Start at the front of the head and work back. Shade in one side of each chest feather.

Shade the feathers and darken the shadowed parts.

Drawing feathers

All feathers follow the same basic shape. Start by drawing the broad flat outline. Draw a long shaft down the middle of the feather.

Sketch in the delicate barbs that run off the shaft. Hold a piece of paper along the shaft, so that your strokes can go right up to the line but not over it.

Now fill in the barbs on the other side of the feather. Use the piece of paper again to make sure the lines don't run over the middle shaft.

Finally, use the edge of a pointed eraser to create highlights. Sweep the eraser down the length of your feather to give the impression of a glossy sheen.

Flickering flight

Fold a small sheet of paper in half.

Trace a bird from below on to the top right-hand area of the bottom page.

Trace the other bird in exactly the same place on the front page.

OOPS! To make sure the bird's flight is smooth, tape the paper to the window and line up the heads and feet.

Flick the top page very fast and watch your bird fly!

18

This feather is sleek, shiny and tapered.

This rounded feather is brown and mottled.

Peacock feathers are like jewelled eyes.

Long, swirly feathers are found in birds' tails.

Small, soft, downy feathers keep birds warm.

Sketch book

It's a hoot!

Jeepers peepers! Learn how to draw this wide-eyed owl in a knotty tree house, before she flies off to hunt for supper.

You'll need a 2B pencil, sharpener, eraser, a fine black felt-tip pen and colored pencil.

Twit-twoo! Here's a wise, saw-whet owl sitting in her favorite tree. You'll need a soft pencil to create the dark textures of her woody lair. She has huge, round eyes which help her to see while hunting at night. Leave a dot of white in the pupils for a really scary glare. Shade the feathers fanning out from the eyes into a soft ruff and curve them downwards to overlap the legs. For a contrast to the soft feathers, draw the curvy bark shapes with circular, shaded lines around her black, tree-hole home.

UN ACTS Owls are found all over the world, mostly in woodlands. There are over 145 different types. These vary in size from the elf owl in the southwest, which is a weeny 6 inches long, to the great grey owl in Canada which is 30 inches in length! Owls are nocturnal birds – this means that they hunt at night and sleep during the day. Their large eyes cannot move in their sockets, so owls move their whole heads around to watch their prey. Because of these curious habits and their wise expressions, owls have often been regarded as mysterious birds and have appeared in many myths and legends. The Ancient Greeks believed that owls were sacred to Athena, their goddess of wisdom.

ha ha!

Why did the owl need a towel?

He was too wet to woo!

...now draw it step by step

1 Sketch a bean-shaped face in the top half of the page. Draw two round eyes inside this. Add a tiny, pointed beak at the bottom of the bean shape.

2 Dot a mask shape around the eyes. Shade the pupils, leaving a white dot. Draw the body and little wings. Sketch two, short legs ending in claws.

3 Shade a dark, oval hole around the owl. Start to draw short lines for feathers – make them darkest around the beak. Begin outlining the bark.

4 For head feathers, draw groups of lines pointing from the owl's eyes towards the edge of the face. Crosshatch the bark around the hole.

5 Finish shading the owl's body. Scribble lines for ruffled feathers, curving them down to the legs. Add more bark lines. Shade the claws.

Quickdra
...a mouse

This nervous wood mouse ha
keep an eye out for hunting c

Draw an oval for the head. Ad
larger oval behind it with a fla
bottom edge, for the body.

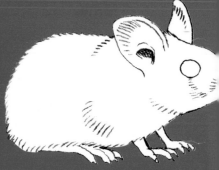

Reshape the head and body.
large ears. Sketch a circle for
eye and a tiny, curved nostr

Sketch fur lines around the ou
cheeks and in the ears. Add do
the nose. Draw the legs and f

Draw a curved, ridged tail. Sh
the eye, leaving a white highli
Sketch the whiskers and more

Sketch book

Chirpy chicks

Get off to a flying start and sketch these hungry baby birds in a nest!

You'll need a 2B and 4B pencil, sharpener, eraser, paintbrush, paints and a black felt-tip pen.

These chicks can't wait to be fed! Baby birds automatically open their beaks wide when they see the shape of a parent bird approaching. They know that dinner's on the way! Shade the gaping mouths of the chicks and use short pencil strokes for their feathery down. With a 4B pencil, shade a dramatic, dark background. The pale leaves help to frame the picture and lots of interwoven lines make up their comfy nest. Now it's time for you to get weaving!

FUN FACTS

Nearly all birds incubate their eggs by sitting on them. Their body heat keeps the eggs warm and allows the chicks to develop inside. Often, the parents take turns sitting on the eggs. When most chicks are born they are blind and featherless and their legs are too weak to support their bodies. Young birds learn to fly without needing to be taught. When they are strong enough to try, they will stand on the edge of their nest to stretch their wings. They practice their flying skills by making short, clumsy trial runs. It can take months of practice before they are ready to take off!

ha ha!
How do birds dance?
Chick-to-chick

21

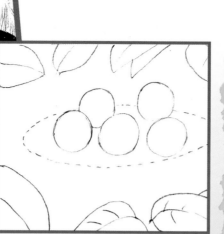

Dinner's ready! The mother
has found a juicy earthwor
feed her hungry chicks.

...now draw it step by step

1 To frame the picture draw leaves at the top and bottom. Draw five circles for the birds' heads in the center. Lightly sketch an oval around these.

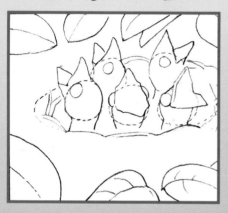

2 Add the beaks and sketch circular, bulging eyes on each head. Draw the twigs at the top of the nest, erasing the guideline as you go.

3 Draw narrow pupils, leaving out tiny white highlights. Shade inside the beaks. Start drawing head feathers and build up the nest with twigs.

4 Finish shading the heads. Draw more twigs weaving in and out on the nest. Add a leaf stalk. Then, shade the leaves and inside and under the nest.

5 Shade the bottom of the nest with crosshatching. Finish shading the birds' down and feathers. With a 4B pencil, darkly shade the background.

For the bird's body, sketch a slightly bulging oval. Add a head on top and a rectangular tail below.

Draw an eye. Add the top part of the beak, extending into the head. Build up the wing with short curves.

Add the bottom beak and a worm with tiny ridges to make it look round. Draw wing and tail details and a foot gripping a branch.

Shade the front of the head and lower belly with short pencil strokes. Leave the chest, back, tail and a line under the head white.

DRAWING ✓
SHADING ✓

Dashing dolphins

You'll need a 2B pencil, ruler, eraser and sharpener!

You can draw this splashy picture of racing dolphins using shading to show the speedy creatures leaping out of the waves.

Dolphins love to chase after boats on the high seas. The smooth curves and shiny skin of these wonderful, leaping creatures are drawn with long lines of shading along their backs. The rushing waves they make as they speed through the water are also made with lots of long shading lines. These create the sort of blurred effect you get when you take a photograph of a moving object.

ha ha!
Where do dolphins live exactly?
The Specific ocean!

FUN FACTS

Dolphins are not fish, but mammals. They breathe air through blowholes on the top of their heads and are warm-blooded like humans. Like whales, dolphins are kept warm by a thick layer of fatty blubber below their skin. Blubber also acts as a storage place for food.

Dolphins can track down objects underwater using echolocation, a natural sonar system. By making a series of clicking sounds, which produce echoes when they bounce off things in a dolphin's path, the creature can work out what lies ahead.

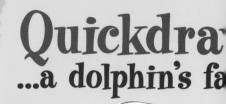

Quickdraw
...a dolphin's fa

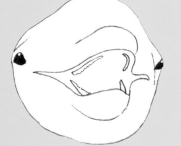

Draw a circle. Add two curv
to shape the dolphin's hea
and two small ovals for eye

...now draw it step by step

1 Sketch three fish shapes, one above the other. Draw the whole bodies for the top two dolphins, and just the head for the bottom one.

2 Make the noses more beak-shaped and add fins. Draw a line from the dolphins' beaks to the flippers. Add the eyes and some splashes.

3 Draw in smiley mouths. Add long shading lines along the backs leaving a white highlight in the middle. Shade the eyes and flippers.

Sketch in curves for the mouth, nose and chin. Add teeth and darken the eyes.

Shade inside the mouth an around the face leaving an arrow shape on the forehea

4 Draw long shading lines in a diagonal direction in the water. This gives a feeling of the dolphin whizzing through it. Add the dolphins' markings.

5 Shade the water in the dolphins' shadow. Give the picture perspective by shading short, horizontal lines to show the distant sea.

Shade rings of rippling wate around the dolphin to add feeling of movement.

DRAWING ✓
PAINTING ✓
MASKING ✓

Sea cow WOW!

Sketch this manatee mom swimming with her cute and curious baby!

You'll need a 2B pencil, ruler, eraser and sharpener!

Manatees, also known as sea cows, are gentle sea creatures that fishermen once believed were mermaids!

Sketching the manatee shapes is easy, but they need some careful cross-hatch shading to make them look round and chubby! The rippled surface of the water above the animals is created with swirls of circular shading. Down below, around their bellies and paddle-like flippers, the water is dark and shadowy. Follow the steps over the page and have fun drawing this playful pair!

FUN FACTS

Manatees are big on grazing (which is why they are also called sea cows) and can gobble as much as 100 pounds of water plants every day. Sometimes, they are even used as underwater mowers to keep rivers weed-free! Manatees weigh up to 2,000 punds and grow to 10ft long. They move slowly through the water and surface every 10 to 15 minutes for air. There are three different types of manatee - the African manatee which lives in the sea, the Amazon manatee which lives in the Amazon river, and the Caribbean manatee which is found in sea bays and rivers. All are endangered as they've been hunted for their meat, skin and oil.

ha ha!
What does a manatee drink when it's hot? A mug-a-tea!

...now draw it step by step

1 For the basic body shapes, draw two ovals at an angle. It's best to draw these lines faintly as you might need to erase them later.

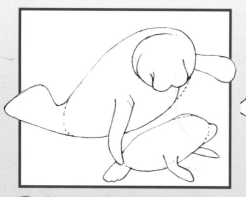

2 Sketch the flippers and tails. Add the baby's head and nose. Then draw curves for the mother's head with a rounded W for her muzzle.

3 Add small eyes and detail on the faces. Shade heavily on the flippers and under the bodies. Begin to shade rings around the manatees' bodies.

4 Use crosshatching to make the shadows darker. Add more detail to the faces. Shade on the manatees' backs, where the light hits them.

5 Shade circular ripples above the manatees and add crosshatching below them. Use an eraser to erase highlights and wrinkles.

26

Quickdra ...a piranha

This fierce fish lives in th Amazon, alongside the gentle manatee.

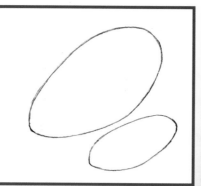

Draw a lop-sided oval.

Add a humped back, a ta stump, a mouth and the curve of the head.

Draw the fins, a tail, an ey in a socket and teeth. Ad wrinkles around the head a shade inside the mouth.

Draw some overlapping scales. Shade short lines around the head to make it look solid.

DRAWING ✓
SHADING ✓
PAINTING ✓

Ray okay

Sunlight creates patterns on the ocean bed, as a huge manta ray glides gracefully by. Find out how to sketch this marvellous, marine scene.

You'll need a 2B and 4B pencil, sharpener and eraser

Silently sliding through the water, the manta ray moves with gentle strokes of its huge fins. Although it looks scary, it only eats minute sea creatures and plants, called plankton. The large, bendy lobes on either side of its head are used to help fan these into its mouth. Build up the ray's shape with several layers of crosshatching. Gently smudge shadows on the ocean floor, then use the sharp edge of a clean eraser to erase wavy lines for a fab, sun-dappled effect.

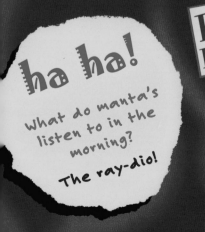

ha ha!

What do manta's listen to in the morning?

The ray-dio!

FUN FACTS There are more than 300 species of ray. Most of them feed on small fish, worms and shellfish. They have little teeth which they use to grind the shells. Rays hide from predators by fanning their wide pectoral fins to make hollows in the sand, then burrowing down until only their eyes are above the surface! The smallest ray is the stingray – at 15 inches long, it may seem easy prey, but the poisonous sting at the end of its tail keeps attackers at bay. The giant manta ray can grow up to 23 feet in length and weigh up to 3,500 pounds. When it picks up speed, it can leap up to 5 feet out of the water!

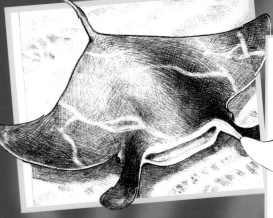

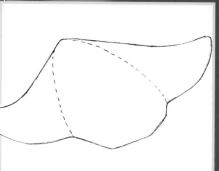

...now draw it step by step

Lightly sketch an upside-down shield shape which leans to the left. Add bendy triangles on either side of the body for the ray's giant fins.

Flying fish are another spe
that can leap right out of
water. Just look at their f

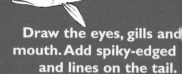

Start by drawing a long o
for the fish's body, with
tail fin on the right.

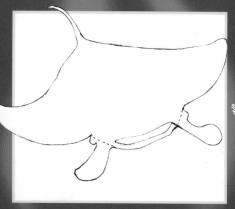

2 Draw a wide mouth at the front, with flapping lobes on each side. Sketch a bulging eye at the top of each lobe. Add a thin, curved tail.

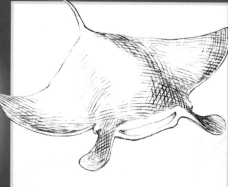

3 Begin crosshatching with long, curved pencil strokes, following the ray's shape. Carefully build up several layers with a 4B pencil.

Draw the eyes, gills and mouth. Add spiky-edged and lines on the tail.

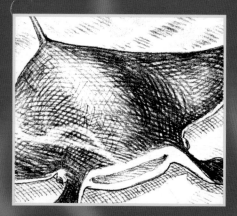

4 Crosshatch the ray's shadow and ripples on the sand. Smudge these with your finger. Use the point of an eraser to erase lines on the ray's back.

5 Finish erasing the wavy lines on the sea bed to create the effect of dappled sunlight. Make sure that you don't erase the ray's shadow.

Draw the wing-like fins o
either side of the fish. Ad
detail to the head.

Sketch crisscross lines fo
scales and shade them ligh
Shade the wings and face

Sketch book

You'll need a 2B pencil, eraser, sharpener, scissors, paper and household objects for rubbing.

Scaly fish

Something fishy is going on around here! Learn how to make this fantastic underwater picture with clever shading and rubbing tricks.

Fish have lots of scales all over their bodies and drawing them all would not be possible! But you can create some realistic-looking fish scales with a clever shortcut called textured rubbing (it's also known as frottage). To make your own amazing undersea world full of scaly creatures, just follow the easy steps on the next two pages. Frottage is a fast, fun way of making a picture.

FUN FACTS

Fish come in all shapes and sizes. The largest fish in the world is the whale shark - some sharks can grow up to 59 feet long, that's twice the length of a bus! The tiniest sea fish is the dwarf goby - it swims around in the Indian Ocean and is small enough to fit on a finger-nail. Fish have some extraordinary ways of dealing with their enemies. Some fish send out electrical pulses to kill prey or communicate with other sea creatures. The most powerful electric fish is the electric eel. Puffer fish can inflate into a balloon shape by swallowing water or air when enemies approach!

ha ha!

Why are fish good at music?

They practice their scales.

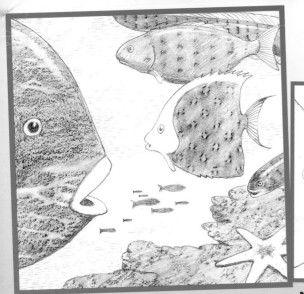

...now draw it step by step

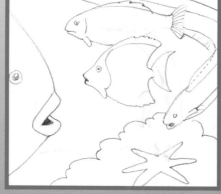

1 Draw a large curve at the left edge of the paper, with two tiny circles for the fish's eye. Make a cloud shape at the bottom for the coral.

2 Next, draw the big fish's mouth and a star shape on the coral. Start with half an oval for the little fish and add eyes, mouth, tail and fins.

Finish off the starfish's body. Next, draw the long fish and the eel. Draw the eel's body first, then add the fin along its back.

3

4 Rub textures on to the fish and the coral, as explained opposite. Don't be afraid to go over the lines – you can clean up later with an eraser.

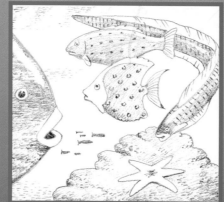

5 After rubbing on the textures, add the tiny fish and some horizontal lines for the water. Add highlights on the fish and shafts of light with an eraser.

Quickdra ...fish

● **To draw this jellyfish start with an oval and add lots of wavy tentacles.**

● **This fish has scary teeth and big lips. Don't forget the fine lines in the fins and tail.**

● **This eel is shaped like the letter S, with fins all the way down the top and bottom edges.**

● **To make a stingray look solid, add a curl on the wing.**

● **To draw this fish, start with half an oval. Add fins, mouth and tail.**

Make ...rubbings

ll sorts of household odds and nds have textured surfaces hat make great rubbings. Look r things that are rough or tterned. You can use a grater, brick, a piece of wood, a eet of coarse sandpaper, or n the bottom of your shoe!

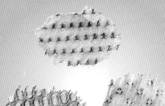

ese rubbings are from a grater!

of a
shoe

Glass dish

File

Place your paper over a xtured object.
Using the side of a sharp, soft ncil, rub over the object.
Don't press too hard with the ncil, or you'll pierce the paper.
Keep the paper still when u are rubbing the object derneath it.

Top textures

You can make textured rubbings using wax crayons, pastels, colored pencils and charcoal. Look around the house or garden for objects – those with a clear outline work best. You can make some fantastic textured rubbings with coins, keys, shells and fossils. Start to build up a collection of objects that you can rub.

Color work

To make a leaf rubbing, turn the leaf over with the smooth side down. Lay a sheet of paper over the leaf and rub firmly with a crayon. If you attach the stalk to the paper with a little bit of sticky tape, it will help keep the leaf still as you work. Rubbing the leaf with two different crayons creates a great effect!

Sketch book

Shark attack!

You'll need a 2B and 6B pencil, eraser, sharpener, black felt-tip pen and colored pencils.

Swim for your life! This man-eating shark seems to be leaping right out of the page. Find out how to draw your own fearsome fish!

As this scary shark crashes to the surface, it reveals rows of razor-sharp teeth inside its huge jaws. Has the creature spotted a victim to snap up? The shark's light, shiny head contrasts with the dark inside of its mouth, which you can create with careful crosshatching. The shading gets darker behind the teeth and at the back of the throat. Make the big water splashes look foamy with some soft shading. Now, grit your teeth and dive into some drawing!

FUN FACTS Although sharks have a reputation for being fierce, they probably attack fewer than 100 people every year. Most sharks are too busy hunting for other fish to bother with humans! These huge, meat-eating fish have excellent hearing and vision, and they don't have to worry about losing teeth – when one falls out, a new tooth simply moves forward to take its place! In a lifetime, a shark can go through thousands of teeth, which they most definitely need because they are massive eaters.

ha ha!
What do you call a fish with no eyes?
Fsh!

...now draw it step by step

1 Sketch the cone-shaped shark's head with a wavy line below. Pencil in the mouth outline. This is almost square with a curved, bottom edge.

2 Reshape the left side of the head. Draw a tiny eye and nostril. Inside the mouth, add a gum line with rows of teeth and short, curved lines for gills.

3 Draw short lines for wrinkles on the nose and texture on the gums. Shade the tip of the nose. Sketch an outline for the splashing water.

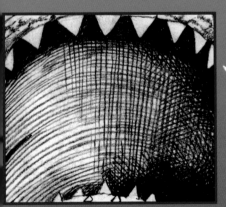

4 Draw curves round the inside of the mouth. Then, crosshatch with downward lines. Shade heavily around the teeth and back of the throat.

5 Shade below the mouth. Use a soft pencil to shade ripples around the splashes. Add short lines and dots on the splashes for light texture.

Quickdraw
...a shark

Sketch this super shark swimming silently through the sea.

Start by sketching a long leaf shape with an open end for the shark's body.

Add the mouth, eye and nostril. Draw triangular dorsal and tail fins.

Pencil in the side pectoral fins. Draw a wavy line along the body and four gill slits.

Shade under the body with curved lines. Add patches of shading on the side and fins.

33

Super sharks!

There are about 370 different species of shark. Some are long, thin and pointy, others have strange-shaped heads and sharp-edged fins. Here are a few of these amazing creatures.

Great white shark
This fast, powerful shark is pret dangerous. It kills i prey by taking a bi and wildly shaki its hea

Whale shark
This shark can grow up to 40 ft long and weigh twice as much as an elephant, but it only feeds on tiny fish and plankton!

Hammerhead shark
No prizes for guessing how this fish got its name! Th hammerhead may look b and scary, but it is ofte shy around human

Hornshark
This shark is also known as the pig shark because of its ugly-looking snout! Its teeth are made up of cutters and crushers so it can munch on shellfish.

Leopard shark
This spotty creature live on the ocean floor and feed on small sea animals. It will no attack unless provoked

Make it gory!

Why not color your shark using colored pencil? Sketch the outline of your picture and go over it with black felt-tip pen. Color the inside of the mouth with different shades of pink, red and purple. Build up extra texture with small areas of grey and black. Use greens and blues to color in the sea. Finally, lightly shade the water splashes with pale blues and greens.

Snap to it!

You'll need a 2B pencil, eraser, fine black felt-tip pen, fine paintbrush and watercolor paints.

This gruesome alligator is feeling mighty hungry. Grab a pencil and have fun doing a scary, scaly sketch!

Draw this ravenous reptile as it lies on the riverbank, ready to snap up passing prey. The corners of the alligator's mouth are turned up like a smile, but its powerful jaws and razor-sharp teeth are no laughing matter! The patterned, scaly skin on its sides is made up of lots of tiny squares which fit together perfectly, but the scales on its face are uneven. The ridges along its back are drawn with spiky, zigzag lines. You can really get your teeth into this snappy sketch!

FUN FACTS

Alligators, crocodiles, caymans, and gavials belong to a group of reptiles known as crocodilians. There are about 23 different species of crocodilians altogether. They have been around for 140 million years and are probably the closest living relatives to the dinosaur! Alligators' skins are very tough, with tiny bones forming ridges along their backs. They swim by moving their long, heavy tails from side to side in the water and feed on small animals like fish, snakes, frogs and turtles. The victims are dragged underwater by the fearsome reptiles. Alligators have been known to attack dogs, pigs and cattle, too!

ha ha!
What happened when the alligator ate a comedian?
He felt funny!

...now draw it step by step

1 Sketch a long, flat oval at an angle for the alligator's body. Add a long, curved tail at the top end to get the basic alligator shape.

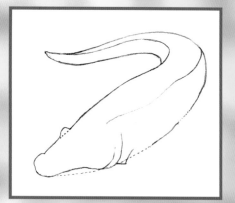

2 Add shape to the body by drawing a snout and the bulge of the eye and the jaw. Draw lines to separate the alligator's back from its sides.

3 Draw a wavy line for the mouth, an eye, three legs and clawed feet. Add long ridges running down the alligator's back.

4 Make the ridges look spiky with zigzag lines. Crosshatch over the alligator's sides and legs for a scaly effect. Add detail to the face.

5 Draw the water's edge and shade reflections with vertical lines. Draw the tree root in the background and add detail to the bank.

Draw a long sha with a po at the top and a hook at the bottom

Draw in the head around the point, with a bulging eye and a slightly open mouth. Draw thin legs and clawed feet at the front.

Add the back legs with webbed feet. Draw ridges on the tail and cross-hatching for the scales. Outline the teeth.

Shade inside the mouth. Finish adding texture to the scaly body. Shade circular ripples on the surface of the water.

Happy snappers

Can you tell a croc from an alligator? Do you know when you're being glared at by a gavial? Study up on these scary species with this guide to gnashing, thrashing reptiles.

Crocodiles

Crocodiles have longer, narrower snouts than alligators. They also have terrible teeth! The fourth tooth on each side of the lower jaw sticks out over their top jaw when their mouths are closed.

Alligators

Alligators have chunkier heads than crocodiles and only their top teeth show when their mouths are closed. When they are wet, their skin looks almost black.

Gavials

Gavials are found in India. They have bulging eyes and narrow snouts which are perfect for catching fish. Their teeth slot together like a zip, making sure nothing escapes!

Practice your scales!

The scales on a crocodile's belly and sides are large, smooth squares. The scales on its back are made up of lots of small circles. They fit together like a suit of green armour all over its body. To color a crocodile, draw the outline of each scale using a fine, black felt-tip pen. When the pen is dry, brush over the scales using pale yellow watercolor paint. Once dry, paint the gaps between the square scales dark green. Finally, dot different shades of green on to the rough scales on the crocodile's back.

Sketch book

Dragon flight

You'll need a 2B pencil, a sharpener and an eraser.

People have been telling myths and tales about dragons for a long time. But all dragons – firebreathing or friendly – are fun to draw.

This magnificent dragon is easier to draw than it looks.

● Start with the body and the head and then add the wings and tail.

● After that, you can gradually start to build up the layers of scales

● To help you draw the scales you can use guidelines.

● No one knows what color dragons actually were, so you can really let your imagination fly when you start coloring in!

FUN FACTS

Dragons were mythical creatures. According to legends they lived in remote, wild regions, terrorizing local villages. But they weren't all bad. The Chinese believe that dragons were god-like creatures and, according to the Chinese calendar, people who are born in the year of the dragon are lucky and powerful. The only known dragons alive today are the Komodo Dragons of Indonesia. These aren't real dragons at all, but enormous flesh-eating lizards, which got their name from their amazing size - they can grow to over 29 feet in length!

ha ha!
What does a dra
eat after it's h
a tooth out
The dentis

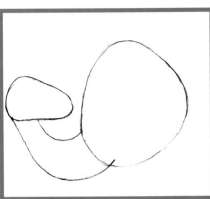

...now draw it step by step

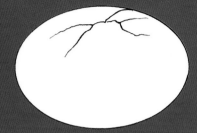

Quickdraw
...a baby dragon

Start with an oval for the egg and draw a crack in the top.

1 Start with rough outlines for the main shapes. First, draw an oval for the dragon's body. Draw in another oval for the head. Join the head and the body with a long, thick neck.

At first, all that pokes out of the egg is the dragon's snout.

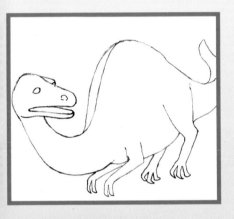

2 Draw in the mouth, nostril and eyes and add the dragon's tail and legs. Add a line along the center of the back. This will show you where the dragon's spines and wings go.

3 Next, add the wings and the spines along the dragon's back. Draw in his horns, his ears and his lolling tongue! Fill in his eye and nostril. Then add creases to the underside of his body.

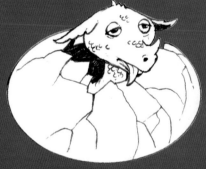

Draw the dragon's sleepy head. Add more cracks and shade in the hole.

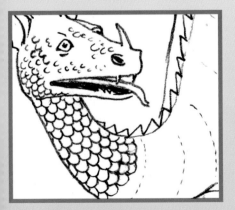

4 Draw in dotted guidelines that follow the curves of the body. Start drawing in the scales. Make them bigger as you move down the neck.

5 Continue drawing in the scales – they are biggest in the middle of the body. Watch out for the dragon's legs – the scales change direction here.

Draw your hatched dragon sitting down. Finally, make the egg look broken.

Scaly skills

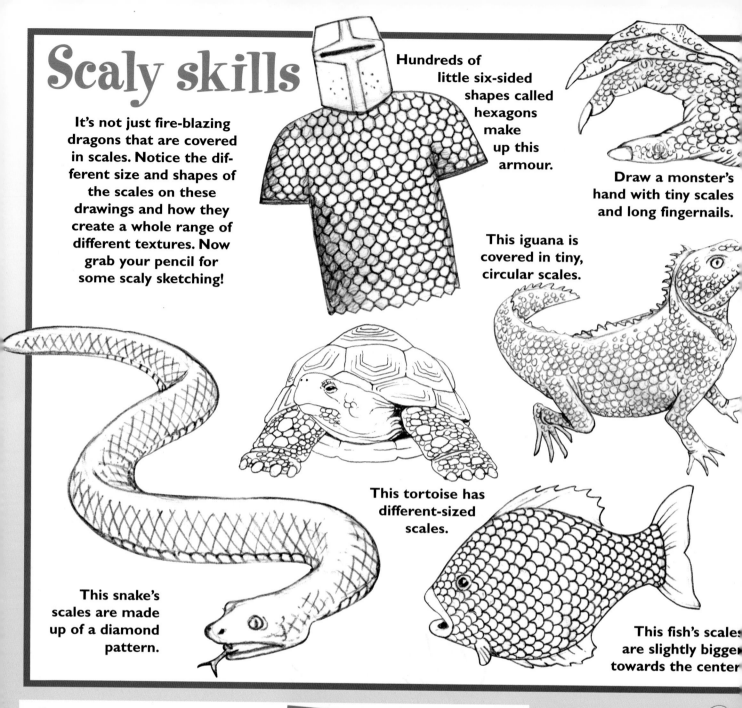

It's not just fire-blazing dragons that are covered in scales. Notice the different size and shapes of the scales on these drawings and how they create a whole range of different textures. Now grab your pencil for some scaly sketching!

Hundreds of little six-sided shapes called hexagons make up this armour.

Draw a monster's hand with tiny scales and long fingernails.

This iguana is covered in tiny, circular scales.

This tortoise has different-sized scales.

This snake's scales are made up of a diamond pattern.

This fish's scales are slightly bigger towards the center.

Color them in

Once you've drawn in your scales, you can make them more interesting with some color and shading. For example, when you draw the snake, add highlights by leaving the scales off the top. Shade the scales on the sides of the snake. The shading should become darker towards the bottom. You can use different colors for the different shades, too.

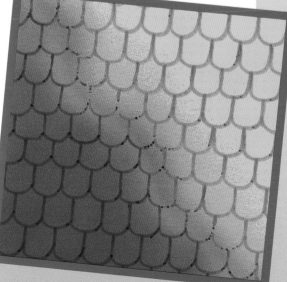

Link up!

A knight's armor was called chain mail, and was made up of small chains linked together. To draw a chain, start with a row of ovals, making every other oval narrower and taller. Shade them where they link.

Part 2

Drawing Scary Stuff, Speed and Space

Sketch book

Scary bats!

Drawing a bat isn't as frightening as it looks! Follow these simple steps to sketch this creepy creature!

You'll need a 2B pencil, eraser, sharpener and white paper!

Look closely at this bat – it looks a bit like a flying mouse! The trick to drawing it is to make the body look furry and the wings leathery. Notice the bat's large ears. These are designed to make its hearing super sensitive so it can track prey as it flies through the night. Use crisscross lines for the sky to contrast with the markings on the bat.

FUN FACTS Bats are the only mammals that can fly, but their wings are covered with thin skin, not feathers. There are over 900 types of bats. The largest is the flying fox, which has a wingspan of 6 feet. The smallest is the Kitti's hog-nosed bat, which is the size of a bumble bee! Bats live all over the world, except in very cold places. Most bats sleep all day hanging upside down in places like caves, attics and sheds. They only come out to feed at night. Lots of people are afraid of bats, even though they are pretty harmless! The vampire bat in South America does feed on blood - but only from animals! Other bats prefer fruit and insects.

ha ha! Which bats are good at gymnastics? Acrobats!

...now draw it step by step

1 Draw the basic shapes of the body and wings. Notice that the bat's right wing is a bit longer due to the angle it has been drawn from.

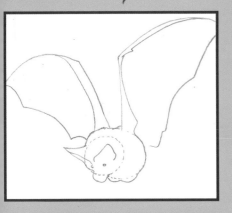

2 Add the head details to the basic body shape (shown with dotted lines). Carefully draw the wings with a double line where they fold over.

3 Add the leg and the 'tail' area around it. Draw the fine 'finger' bones in the wings. Shade the body with short strokes to create a furry effect.

4 Shade the wings with long strokes. Make the shading dark in places to suggest movement. Draw the outlines of the clouds and the moon.

5 Draw crisscross lines for the sky, leaving spaces for stars. Lightly shade the clouds, leaving the edge nearest the moon white for a moonlit effect.

Quickdraw
...a bat

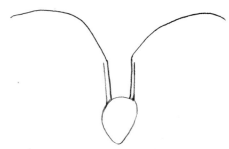

Draw an oval for the body and curved lines for the wings.

Add large ears and a pointy chin. Draw the wings. Break up the outline of the body to make it look furry.

Draw the fierce-looking face. Add lines to the wing structure.

Shade the face with short strokes. Make the fur on the body longer. Add lots of short lines to the wings to make them look leathery.

Sketch book

Fierce fangs!

You'll need a 2B pencil, sharpener, eraser, small glass or other round object and ruler (optional).

Yikes! This wolf looks really fierce, but it's fun to draw! Here's how to make your creepy picture a howling success!

This scary, wild wolf isn't as frightening to sketch as it looks! Draw the creature's head very carefully using short, stiff lines for the fur. Make sure that they all follow the shape of the head. The background is easy. Draw round a small glass or other round object for the moon and use dark scribble shading for the pine trees. The night sky is drawn with lots of crisscross lines – you can use a ruler if you like. This helps to give the scene a dark, spooky atmosphere.

FUN FACTS

Wolves are dog-like animals found in remote parts of Europe, Asia and North America. There are two main species, the grey or timber wolf and the red wolf. They live in family groups called packs. Wolves are expert hunters, preying mainly on large animals such as caribou, deer, elk and moose. In ancient times, wolves were much more common, but people have destroyed them in large numbers because they sometimes kill farm animals. People also think that wolves attack humans and are frightened by their howling. But wolves are more scared of people and avoid them as much as possible.

ha ha!
Why did the wo
put a box ove
its head?
Because it wa
to hunt i
a pack

Quickdraw
...a howling wolf

Draw two rough circles and an oval for the wolf's body. Add a base for it to sit on.

Draw the outline of the wolf by connecting the shapes, then add the leg, tail and jaws.

Rough up the outline to make it look furry. Draw round a small, round object for the moon.

Heavily shade the wolf all over, and shade the dark areas of the moon.

...now draw it step by step

1 Draw a large curve and a rough oval overlapping it. These make the basic shapes for the wolf's head, shoulders and muzzle, or snout.

2 Add the pointed, laid back ear, round nose and eye. Draw a large, snarling mouth, set slightly inside the outline of the muzzle.

3 Draw a large fang, the gums and back teeth. Sketch in the face details. Add nostrils to the nose and wrinkles along the muzzle.

4 Add whiskers, dribble and more teeth. Sketch fur with short lines. Use a round object to draw the moon and scribble shade the pine trees.

5 Carefully shade around the jaws with fine, light pencil marks. Finish by filling in the night sky with lots of crisscross lines.

45

Making monsters!

You can make all sorts of creatures look creepy by adding fangs, claws and big tufts of hair!

Crisscross shading under the skull's hood, and dark shading around the eyes makes them really stand out. Spooky!

Try drawing your own hand, then add some claw-like nails and big tufts of hair!

Huge, pointy teeth and strands of saliva make this mouth look truly gruesome!

Draw a basic spider shape, but make it really hairy. Add some extra-long hairs and fangs to make it look totally horrible!

Razor-sharp teeth, claws, a frown and long, thick tail turn a sweet mouse into a nasty rat.

Spooky graveyard

It's dead easy to make this creepy, inky picture! On a sheet of thick, white paper, paint the gravestones and the ground with black, waterproof Indian ink. While it dries, in a saucer mix some dark blue Indian ink, or watercolor paint, with a little water. Then, with a sponge, dab it over the midnight sky. Finally, for a really eerie feel, use a clean sponge to drag a little white paint over the bottom part of the picture. Creepy!

DRAWING ✓
SHADING ✓
HIGHLIGHTING ✓

Draw spooky ghosts

You'll need a 2B pencil, eraser, scissors and sharpener.

Shivering goosebumps! This creepy room is haunted! Find out how to make a ghostly scene using light and shade.

You can use an ordinary eraser to make this ghost, the cobwebs and the patches of spooky moonlight.

Shade the drawing first, with criss-cross pencil strokes – use the side of the pencil for really dark shading. Then simply erase parts of the shading with your eraser. Steps for drawing this picture start on the next page.

To stop your hand smudging the shadows, cover your work with a sheet of white paper as you go.

FUN FACTS

One of the most haunted places in the world is the village of Pluckley, in England, where people have reported seeing at least 12 ghosts. Two of the ghosts, known as the White Lady and the Red Lady, were spotted in the church. At another place called in England, Fright Corner, there's a ghostly highwayman, a screaming man at the brickworks and a spooky coach and horses roaming the village!

ha ha! What's a ghost's favorite food? Spooketti!

Create a ghostly Scene

To make this scary ghost, you'll need to use an eraser as if it was a pencil – so you need to give it a point!

Cut the eraser in half from corner to corner, or ask an adult to help you, to make two triangular pieces.

Use the points to erase thin lines, and the flat sides to lift off larger areas of shading.

When your eraser gets dirty, rub it clean on a piece of spare paper.

...Now draw it step by step

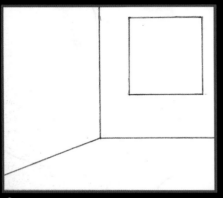

1 Start with a square in the top, right corner for the window. Then draw lines from the top, the left and the right edges of the paper for the walls.

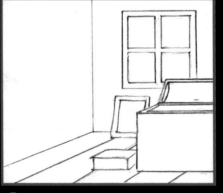

2 Now add some detail. Draw the window frame and treasure chest. Anything you draw on the floor will cast shadows which you'll add later.

3 Draw a moon and fill in the window panes. This is the darkest part of the picture, so make them really black. Add the treasure and other objects.

4 Start shading your picture. Shade one way and then the other to make criss-cross marks. Shade the chest lid from dark to light so it looks curved.

5 Shade more heavily for darker shadows. Notice how the treasure chest and other objects cast shadows on the floor. The far wall is also darker.

6 Use your eraser to add the ghost, moonlight and cobwebs. Leave some shading on them for a see-through effect. Don't forget the ghost's eyes.

DRAWING ✓
SHADING ✓
HIGHLIGHTING ✓

Spooky tree

Watch out! This tree's alive and waiting to grab the next person passing by! Here's how to draw your own creepy tree monster...

You'll need a 2B pencil, eraser, scissors and sharpener.

Have you ever noticed that trees sometimes look like people? The knots and holes in their bark can look like faces. When a tree's branches are bare, they can look like arms with twiggy fingers! Drawing a spooky tree is easy. Start with a basic tree shape, then draw rough bark and an ugly face. To make the picture even more creepy, add some ghostly mist. Erase it with a sharpened eraser – just cut it in half to make a point. To stop your hand smudging the picture, cover your work with a sheet of paper as you go.

FUN FACTS Some trees live to be thousands of years old. The North American bristlecone pine can live up to 4-5,00 years. Oak trees can live to be 1,000 years old or more. THe Big Tree of Lamar, located at Goose Island State Park in Texas, is said to be over 1,000 years old. Legend has it that it was a council tree for the Carancahua Indians and then later for the settlers, The maidenhair tree, or gingko, is the primitive tree on Earth. It has hardly changed in 160 million years and was around when the dinosaurs roamed!

ha ha! Why is a tree surgeon like an actor? Because he's always taking boughs!

...now draw it step by step

1 Draw the basic 'Y' shape of the tree, placing it slightly to the left of your picture. Do two spreading branches, like bent arms with long fingers.

2 Add the face and draw the bark. Make it circle around the eyes to look like wrinkles. Don't make your drawing too dark at this stage.

3 Add some small twigs for the beard and the hair on top of the head. Shade in the eyes, nose and mouth. Draw in a crescent moon shape.

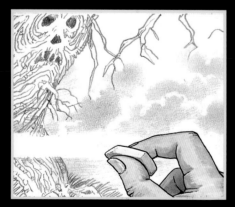

4 Shade in areas of mist and smudge them with a finger. Use the eraser, sharpened to a point, to erase the edges of the clouds and the drifting mist.

5 Shade in the dark sky at the top and smudge it with a finger. If your pencil goes over any of the fine branches, clean them with the sharpened eraser.

Quickdraw
...a tree

Some trees are lollipop-shaped. Try drawing this simple tree.

Lightly draw an outline. Draw the trunk in the middle and an oval for the branches.

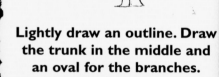

Draw the trunk and main branches, make them thinner at the tips. Erase the outline.

Add lines for the little twigs at the tips of the branches, right to the edge of the outline.

Treetops

All trees have a trunk and branches, but just look at how different they can be! Their leaves are different too.

The horse chestnut is wider at the bottom than at the top. Do you see how the trunk splits quite low down?

With its thick trunk and stubby branches, the baobab looks a bit like a cauliflower floret!

The poplar is very tall and thin, and it's shaped rather like a feather.

The weeping willow has long, floppy branches that reach all the way to the ground.

The spreading branches of the acacia are shaped like an upturned saucer.

FUN FACTS Trees and bushes can be trimmed into all kinds of shapes, animals, birds - even snakes! Training them this way is called topiary.

Barking tips...

Draw wiggly, vertical lines for the simplest kind of bark.

Join the vertical lines and add shading to give the bark more texture.

Where a branch is cut off, the bark forms a spiral-shaped scar.

Smooth bark has hardly any vertical lines, and there are 'eyes' in the bark.

Sketch book

Creepy castle

You'll need a 2B pencil, ruler, eraser, sharpener, small sponge, paintbrush and watercolor paints!

This giant castle in the mountains might be haunted, so take care with your scary shading!

High on a remote mountain stands a mysterious castle. A twisting path winds its way up through the forest to the battlements. Who lives in this spooky spot? And what dark deeds do they get up to in the dingy dungeon? To create this frightening fortress, use a ruler to draw the corner towers (called turrets) and defensive walls. Scribble shade the dark pine trees, and shade the mountain and sky with cross-hatching for a really stormy feel!

FUN FACTS

Before gunpowder was invented in the 14th century, attacking castles was pretty hard work. Because the defensive walls were so huge and strong, armies would often have to hang around outside until they starved the castle owners out! This could take months! Attackers would also use giant catapults to hurl large rocks over the walls at their enemies, or throw a burning mix of tar and sulphur to start fires. In retaliation, castle defenders would fire arrows and drop stones and boiling water down on the invaders.

ha ha! What is the easiest castle to break into? A sand castle!

...now draw it step by step

1 Draw a small, upright rectangle in the center of your paper. Use a ruler to draw six lines for turrets around this. Add a long, snaking path.

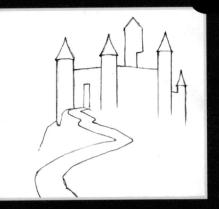

2 Join turrets with straight lines. Sketch spires on each turret. Draw the side of the central tower. Add a tiny turret on the right. Outline the cliff.

3 Finish the central tower. Add two tiny, roofed blocks to the castle. Draw a small turret on the far wall. Outline and scribble shade the trees.

4 Add more shaded trees at the bottom. Darkly shade the right-hand sides of the castle, leaving two windows white. Add detail to the cliff.

5 Outline the mountain with its light edge and lightning bolts above. Crosshatch the dark part of the mountain and patches in the sky.

Lightning bolt!

Paint this striking picture using watercolor paints. Start by filling in the black silhouette of the mountains. Then, use a small sponge to dab on a black and blue night sky, working lightly towards the bottom. Use a fine brush to paint a zigzag line for the main lightning bolt in pale blue. When this is dry, paint a thin white line over it. Finally, add some finer, white zig-zags in the sky.

Quickdraw
...a gargoyle

Look up and you'll see plenty of gargoyles on ancient castle walls!

Draw a straight line down and half a pointy head shape with a rounded triangle ear on the left-hand side.

Add a horn, eye, nostril and mouth with a fang. Add details to the ear, forehead and around the eye.

Trace the left half. Flip over the tracing paper and draw over the outline again to transfer the right side. Lightly outline shading areas.

Crosshatch the shadowy areas on the right of the face and in the ears and horns. Add dots to give a stony texture.

Dark dungeon

In the lower reaches of the sinister castle there is a collection of eerie objects for you to sketch!

Fired up
Crosshatch around the flame on this wall torch to create a smoke effect. Add curved shading on both sides of the handle.

Skull skill
Knock! Knock! Loosely crosshatch the wooden background this skull knocker hangs on. Then shade around the skull's eyes and forehead.

Flame on
Carefully sketch short lines along the left side of each drip of candle wax. Alternate columns of dark and light shading around the base of the candlestick.

Lock wise
Castle doors need big keys! Give this bunch a dotty texture to make them look rusty and old.

Chalice cheat
To draw this shiny chalice, you could sketch one side and use tracing paper to transfer the other to match!

Chunky chain
Build up the links of this chain with a series of overlapping ovals. Gradually draw each link in the chain at a slightly different angle and shade with short, curved lines.

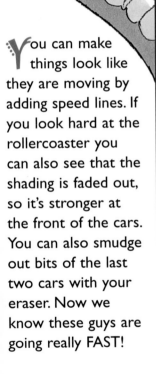
Sketch book

Fast forward

Do you love those theme park rides? When you draw moving objects do you want them to look really exciting? Here's how to get that sense of speed.

You'll need a 2B pencil, eraser, sharpener, ruler and whatever you like to color with!

You can make things look like they are moving by adding speed lines. If you look hard at the rollercoaster you can also see that the shading is faded out, so it's stronger at the front of the cars. You can also smudge out bits of the last two cars with your eraser. Now we know these guys are going really FAST!

FUN FACTS

The fastest moving thing isn't a racing car, an airplane or a spaceship - it's light! You can't see light moving, but it can travel from its source at 186,282 miles per second! Nothing is faster than that. Sound also moves very fast. At 0°C, it can travel through air at 1,085 feet per second, and gets faster as temperatures rise. Some jet planes can fly faster than sound. This is called breaking the sound barrier and causes a noise like a thunderclap, called a sonic boom. In 1997, a special car driven at 1,118 feet per second across the Nevada desert was the first land vehicle to break the sound barrier.

ha ha!
What's the fastest breed of dog?
The dash hound!

...now draw it step by step

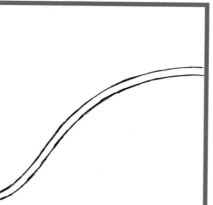

1 Carefully draw two curves side by side for the track of the rollercoaster. You could use a plate to help you.

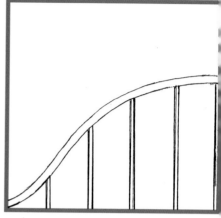

2 With a ruler draw four pairs of lines below your curves as supports for the ride. Make them equal distances apart.

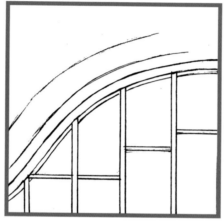

3 Add a few supports going across. Then lightly draw two guidelines where the cars of the rollercoaster will go.

4 Draw the bodies of the cars between the guidelines, with the backs of the seats above. Add some diagonal supports.

Special tips
...for speed

Think of all the things around you that move and use speed lines to make your drawings of them look real. In each of the pictures on the right things move in a different way, some in straight lines, some spinning round and round. Make your lines match what they do.

Use a plate to help you draw curved speed lines. Imagine that the lines continue around the back of the spinning feet.

Eeks! Scary!

See how you can make the passengers on the rollercoaster look really SCARED! Draw their eyes and mouth wide open, and make that hair fly out behind them! Add some shading and you're there!

Super speed

If you erase part of your speed lines, you can make things look as if they're moving super fast. Here, lots of pencil lines were used to give the impression that the dragonfly's wings are moving quickly. Then, three vertical curves were highlighted on each wing to get a better effect.

5 Add detail to the cars. Shade under the cars and track. erase the guidelines. Draw the people's bodies, the sea and sails.

6 Now, shade the front of the cars, and add speed lines at the back. Give the people scared faces and fill in the background.

he straight speed lines n the car wheel are dif-rent lengths which help reate the effect of peed.

A few long lines and some short lines across its path make the soccer ball look as if it's flying through the air.

This meteor has extra long speed lines to make it look as if it has come a long way, very fast.

Fast track

You'll need a 2B pencil, ruler, sharpener, eraser, paintbrush and whatever you like to color with!

Get into gear for a thrilling ride in this fantastic Formula One car. Just follow the steps to become fast on the draw!

FUN FACTS Formula One cars can accelerate from 0 to 100 mph and brake back to a standstill in just six seconds! The pressures that drivers feel at top speeds make it difficult for them to move their bodies within the car – like driving with bricks tied to your arms! Not only that, but during a race, drivers can sweat over a quart of water inside their racing suits!

The light is green and they're off! This shiny Grand Prix car leads the race in pole position and the track speeds by in a blur. To make this daredevil driver roar off the page, you'll need to use perspective. Divide your page in half lengthways and mark a point just above the picture called the vanishing point. All the speed lines and angles on the car fan out from this point, giving the picture a feeling of depth. The polished bodywork really seems to gleam with its dark shadows and white highlights. The wide, whizzing wheels are shaded with lots of vertical lines. It's easy to draw this dynamic racer – just let your pencil go for a spin!

ha ha! Which race starts with two people and ends with billions? The human race!

Design
...a helmet

Racing drivers' helmets come in really flashy designs!

Curved highlights round the edges of this helmet make it look shiny.

...now draw it step by step

1 Draw a border. use your ruler to draw a line up the page center to a point 1 inch above the border. This is the vanishing point. Add two lines for the car's front wing.

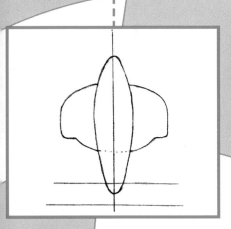

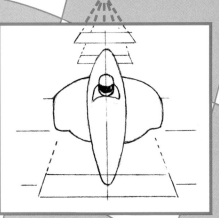

2 Draw a tall oval in the middle of the vertical line, for the car's body. Add matching curved shapes for the car's sides, on either side of the oval.

3 Draw four horizontal lines for rear wings, following ruled lines from the vanishing point. Mark places for the tires. Add the driver.

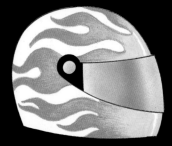

The flames on this hot headgear change gradually from yellow to a fiery red.

A yellow band and strong green stripes make this helmet look really racy!

4 Draw the tires with their treads. Add three air intake holes, two on the sides and one behind the driver. Shade them in. Add curves on the car body.

5 Shade the tires and body. Crosshatch a shadow on the track around the car. Use your ruler to draw the vertical shadow and speed lines from the vanishing point.

Now try designing your own stylish helmet with colored pencils or felt-tip pens.

Pit stop

Formula One racing is very dangerous, so drivers and officials need lots of special gear. Check out what's safe down at the track!

Logo mania
This cap and fireproof racing suit are covered in the names of the driver's sponsors. The suit fits tightly at the neck and has elasticated wrists to keep the driver properly protected.

Head for cover
Under the hard, fibreglass helmet, the driver wears a fire-resistant balaclava which covers all but the eyes.

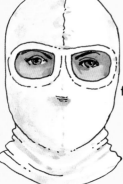

Winning flag
The checkered flag is waved when the winning driver reaches the end of the course. The race official stands on a platform above the track and wears ear protectors.

Hands on
Racers wear big, padded gloves to help them grip the wheel and steer around tight bends.

Get the boot
These purple boots have laces and velcro straps to keep them on tight.

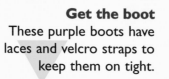

Shine on!

Shiny, polished surfaces can sometimes reflect what is facing them. If the polished area is colored, like the front of this green car, the reflection is colored too and follows the shape of the surface. The silvery chrome on the car's lights and radiator reflects nearby objects. These reflections are a little darker and have a black edge.

Sketch book

Jet away!

You'll need a 2B and 4B pencil, ruler, sharpener, eraser and felt-tip pens.

Strap yourself into the cockpit and take off with this exciting jet plane sketch.

There's a roar in the sky as two modern jet aircraft zoom by. From above, you can see the tops of the clouds and the ground rushing past in a blur. Each jet has a torpedo-shaped body called a fuselage and triangular wings. At the rear, the tailplane is made up of a tail fin with two tinier wings. Shade patches of camouflage on the jet with a very soft pencil, then smudge them with your finger. Use the edge of an eraser to create highlights on the plane and over the tops of the clouds Now, get set for some supersonic sketching!

FUN FACTS Jet engines were first invented in the late 1930s. Hans von Ohain in Germany, and Frank Whittle in Britain, were both working on their own designs, unaware of the other's plans. In August 1939, von Ohain was the first to test his modern engine in a plane. Five years later, both engineers had their designs installed in fighter planes that were battling against each other in the Second World War. After the war, jet engines became even more powerful and, in 1947, pilot Chuck Yeager broke the sound barrier in a specially-built rocket plane. To fly faster than sound, Yeager had to reach a speed of 700 mph. Since then, jets have flown three times as fast as this!

ha ha!
Who has the hardest job on a plane flight?
The window cleaner!

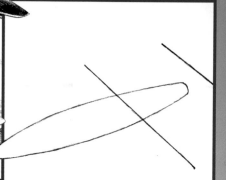

This skydiver has leapt fro
a plane to descend with
rectangular sport parachu

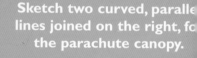

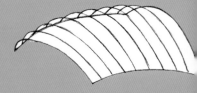

Sketch two curved, paralle
lines joined on the right, fo
the parachute canopy.

**...now draw it
step by step**

Sketch a torpedo shape at an
angle for the fuselage. Use a
ruler to add two diagonal lines
on the right, for the edges of
the wings and tailplane.

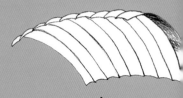

Following the curved line o
the right, draw more curve
between the top and botto

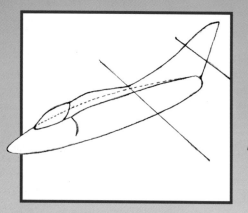

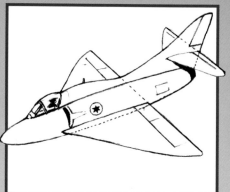

2 Along the top of the fuselage, draw a cockpit at the
front, a hump in the middle
and a tail fin. Add a curve by
the cockpit for the air intake.

3 Draw the front edges and
lines on the wings and
tailplane. Sketch the pilot and
controls in the cockpit, and add
markings on the fuselage.

Draw a skydiver and strap
below the canopy. Begin
shading the canopy stripes

4 Use a 4B pencil to shade
under the tailplane and add
areas of camouflage, smudging
them with your finger. Us your
eraser to create highlights
along the jet's edges.

5 Shade patches of land
below, parallel to the jet's
flight path. Shade clouds above
and draw a second jet. Rub out
highlights behind the jets.

Shade alternate stripes dar
then light. Join the man to t
parachute with straight line

DRAWING ✓
SHADING ✓
COLORING ✓
SPONGE PAINTING ✓

Blast off!

Zoom into outer space with this high-powered spaceship. Then, top off your shading skills with some terrific, extraterrestrial textures!

You'll need white and black paper, 2B and 6B pencils, sharpener, eraser, colored pencils, pieces of sponge, paintbrush, and poster paints!

We have lift off! This rocket is blasting out of the atmosphere. Its matte, metallic surface and white vapor trail make a dramatic contrast to the mysterious patterns on the planet behind it. You'll need a supersoft pencil to create the sensational swirls on this world, and the dense blackness of space. Make the spaceship's body wider at the front, so it really looks as if it's zooming towards you. Follow the cosmic steps over the page, and you'll find it's easy to create your own outer space scene.

FUN FACTS

Our solar system began life as a swirling cloud of dust and gas about 4,600 million years ago. This cloud condensed to form nine planets in an orbit around the sun. Jupiter is the largest planet in the solar system and Pluto is the smallest. The planets closest to the sun are called the inner planets. Earth is one of these. The entire solar system stretches for a massive 7,500 million miles. If you travelled in the type of rocket used to reach the moon in the 1960s, it would take you 86 years to get to Pluto, the planet furthest away from us!

ha ha!
what do you do if you see a spaceman?
Park in it, man!

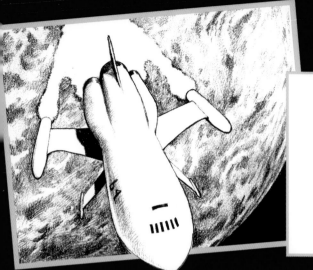

...now draw it step by step

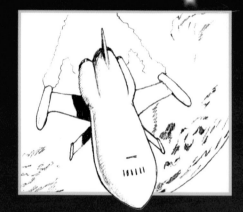

1 Draw a basic rocket shape with three engines at the back. Give it a large pointed nose that breaks out of the picture frame at the bottom.

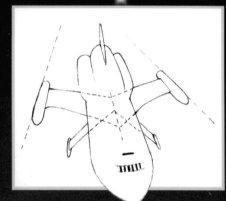

2 Sketch two large and two small wings coming from the sides of the craft at angles. Add a small row of windows at the front and a tail fin.

Shade the craft on the left, leaving a highlighted edge. Add a vapor trail. Draw the planet's curved edge and begin shading patterns on it.

4 Using a 6B pencil, build up the planet's swirly textures. Smudge areas with your finger to create grey tones. Shade outer space to look black.

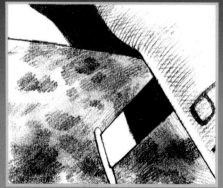

5 Finish shading patches on the planet. Draw a number on the ship's side and use the edge of an eraser to give the highlight a sharp edge.

Quickdra
...an alien

This big-eyed extraterrest comes in peace. Sketch h then take him to your lea

Draw balloo shaped hea and a lon pointe bod

Link the h and body wit neck. D circles for shoulders add thin a and l

Give alien f fingers three te Outline large eyes cheekbo make dots the nostrils a line do the ch

Heav shade th alien's eye one upp arm a below h knees f a rea 3-D E